Thomas Graves Law

A calendar of the English martyrs

Of the sixteenth and seventeenth centuries

Thomas Graves Law

A calendar of the English martyrs
Of the sixteenth and seventeenth centuries

ISBN/EAN: 9783741179518

Manufactured in Europe, USA, Canada, Australia, Japa

Cover: Foto ©Andreas Hilbeck / pixelio.de

Manufactured and distributed by brebook publishing software
(www.brebook.com)

Thomas Graves Law

A calendar of the English martyrs

A CALENDAR

OF THE

ENGLISH MARTYRS

OF THE

SIXTEENTH AND SEVENTEENTH CENTURIES.

LONDON:
ROBSON AND SONS, PRINTERS, PANCRAS ROAD, N.W.

A CALENDAR

OF THE

ENGLISH MARTYRS

OF THE

SIXTEENTH AND SEVENTEENTH CENTURIES.

WITH AN INTRODUCTION

BY

THOMAS GRAVES LAW,
PRIEST OF THE ORATORY.

LONDON: BURNS AND OATES.
1876.

PROTESTATION.

In obedience to the decrees of Pope Urban VIII., I hereby declare that what is stated in this book rests only on human authority, and not on that of the Holy Roman Church, and that it is in this sense only that the name of martyrs is given to those who suffered death for the Catholic faith.

DEDICATED

TO

HER GRACE THE DUCHESS OF NORFOLK,

AT WHOSE REQUEST,

AND WITH WHOSE KIND ASSISTANCE,

THIS CALENDAR OF OUR ENGLISH MARTYRS

HAS BEEN COMPILED.

Sept. 8, 1876.

'Call to mind the former days, wherein, being illuminated, you endured a great fight of afflictions.

'For you both had compassion on them that were in bands, and took with joy the being stripped of your own goods, knowing that you have a better and a lasting substance.'

HEBREWS x. 32, 34.

INTRODUCTION.

———◆———

THE following catalogue of the English martyrs of the six-teenth and seventeenth centuries contains nothing new except the arrangement of the names in the form of a calendar, and perhaps the more exact determination of one or two dates.

It has been drawn up simply for private devotional use. It was thought that such a roll of our martyrs, marking day by day the recurring anniversaries of their victories, would help to keep alive their memory in the minds of English Catholics, and, moreover, suggest the practical devotion of habitually invoking their intercession. Their deaths, pre-cious in the sight of the Lord, have added new glories to the Church militant throughout the world; but we in Eng-land owe to them an especial debt of gratitude. And although in these more peaceful times we may not be called upon to shed our blood for Christ's sake, yet the spirit of martyrdom should never be wanting in us; and the example of the heroic lives, and still more heroic deaths, of these our suffering forefathers in the faith should be continually urging us to a like contempt of this life and this world's goods if set against God's honour.

The Calendar itself is little more than a bare register of names and dates, and was intentionally made as short as possible; but the better to realise its full significance, it may

be well to touch briefly the outlines of the story and the character of the martyrdom which these names recall.

It may be truly said that no country, with perhaps the single exception of Ireland, can boast of so glorious an army of martyrs since the days of the catacombs. The persecution in which they suffered is remarkable for its duration as well as its violence. It commenced with the twenty-seventh year of Henry VIII., and endured with little intermission for about a century and a half until, in 1681, the martyrdom of Oliver Plunket, Archbishop of Armagh, at Tyburn closed the long list which had begun by the execution of the three saintly Carthusian priors and their companions on May 4, 1535. Meanwhile it could reckon among its victims persons of every rank and condition in society—bishops and noblemen; monks and friars, Jesuits and seminary priests, ladies and poor servants, merchants, lawyers, schoolmasters, tradesmen—whose biographies supply us with rare examples of every virtue in every sphere of life, and who, for the most part crowned with the glory of martyrdom, lives already illustrious for eminent sanctity and heroic self-sacrifice.

The particular causes, too, for which these martyrs suffered ought to serve to enhance their merit in our eyes, and render them the dearer to us. Many died in defence of the Catholic doctrine of the Supremacy of the Holy See. This was the cause for which Sir Thomas More, the saintly Bishop of Rochester, the Carthusians, the Bridgettines, the Franciscans and Benedictines, and others, both priests and laymen, gave their lives (eighty-two in all) during the last eight years of Henry's reign. If their number, in comparison with those who fell away at that time, is lamentably small, all the greater honour to the few, who in the face of the national apostasy saw what others were too blind to see, and, like their Divine Master, trod the winepress alone.

The conflict under Elizabeth and in the subsequent period was in some respects of a different nature. In the earlier years of that Queen's reign her Government was content with persecuting measures short of death, hoping by a well-planned system of fines, confiscation, imprisonment, and the gradual extinction of the clergy, little by little to rob the people of England of their newly-recovered faith. And for a while it seemed as if the priesthood must die out, and the Catholic religion in England succumb to heresy without a struggle. It was at this critical moment that, by the forethought and zeal of William Allen, the first English seminary, the fruitful parent of many others and the nursery of future martyrs, was successfully established at Douay. In 1574 a small band of four newly-ordained priests made their way into England. Three years later Cuthbert Mayne, the protomartyr of the seminaries, was hanged, drawn, and quartered at Launceston. Three years more, and no less than a hundred missionaries had poured into the country from Douay, from Rheims, and, from Rome, with marvellous success attending upon their labours. Dr. Allen had now happily persuaded the Society of Jesus to take part in the sacred conflict; and Fathers Campion and Persons entered England in 1580, in which single year it is said that some 10,000 apostates were reconciled to the Church. Meanwhile a succession of sanguinary laws were enacted to meet the reasoning and influence of the new missionaries. It was already a capital crime to maintain the authority of the Pope, to print or publish books maintaining that doctrine, to absolve or reconcile any one to the Church, or to persuade any one to be so reconciled. But this was not enough; and in 1584 the famous Act of the 27th of Elizabeth was passed, by which it was declared high treason for any priest ordained abroad to come into the kingdom; and any one receiving, relieving, or comforting such priest was

to be considered a felon, and to suffer death.   Truly, therefore, has it been said of the clergy of those times that they were martyrs of charity as well as of faith.   English youths, who then voluntarily embraced the ecclesiastical state and the work of a missionary, did so at the risk of their lives for the pure love of souls and with the truest love of country. More than a hundred priests died simply for their sacerdotal character, with no other charge so much as alleged against them than that of offering the Holy Sacrifice; while scores of the laity, with no less zeal and charity, suffered the same punishment for the sole crime of giving aid and shelter to their persecuted pastors.   If among the many martyrs whose names are recorded in the Calendar some were accused of political treason against their sovereign, such accusations were rarely, if ever, believed either by the accusers or the judges who condemned them; and each one of the 260 who suffered death after the accession of Elizabeth might have saved his life by a single visit to the Protestant church.

The following statistics may help to give some idea of how fiercely at times the persecution raged, and how great was the peril incurred by every missionary who ventured upon this glorious strife.   The Douay registers regularly record each year the names of the newly-ordained priests. The list of 1581 gives the ordinations of 43 priests.   Of these 15 are marked with the letter M., as subsequently martyred.   In 1583 the martyrs are 10 out of 29.   Next year they are 9 out of 30, and in 1585 10 out of 24.   During the last six months of a single year, 1588, there were no less than 33 martyrs, 22 of whom were priests.   Yet the stream of missionaries did not slacken.   The report of each fresh martyrdom was celebrated at the college by a Mass of thanksgiving and a solemn *Te Deum*, and only served to stimulate the zeal and fervour of those who were longing to share the same labours and win the same crown.   From

Truly, there-
mes that they
iglish youths,
cal state and
their lives for
e of country.
ir sacerdotal
leged against
while scores
red the same
id shelter to
iartyrs whose
: accused of
accusations
users or the
the 260 who
might have
church.
ome idea of
d how great
10 ventured
rs regularly
ined priests.
priests. Of
ubsequently
29. Next
24. During
rere no less
the stream
each fresh
a Mass of
· served to
longing to
m. From

calculations furnished in 1596 it is estimated that in that year there were already above 300 priests from the seminaries at work on the English mission, assisted by about 50 survivors of the old Marian clergy, and 16 priests of the Society of Jesus.* At this time the catalogue of martyrs already numbered 101 secular priests and 4 Jesuits, while more than 100 priests had been sent into banishment.

During the last years of Elizabeth's reign the Franciscans, following the example already set by the Jesuits, began one by one to enter upon the mission. They in turn were soon followed by the Benedictines, and both now largely helped to swell the list of martyrs. From towards the close of the reign of James I. to the accession of James II. there were occasional periods of comparative rest. The penal laws indeed increased in number and rigour, and the prisons were constantly full, but less blood was actually shed. The reluctance of Charles I. to put priests to death for their religion, it is well known, was one of the chief causes of the rupture between the crown and the parliament which resulted in the rebellion and, with it, a fresh outbreak of violence against Catholics. This continued for some years, and brought a score of priests, regular and secular, to the scaffold. Lastly, after another temporary lull, the excitement produced by the calumnies of Oates awoke the Elizabethan statutes into active operation; and in 1679 the horrors of 1588 were once more repeated, 8 priests of the Society of Jesus, 2 Franciscans, 5 secular priests, and 7 laymen being sacrificed to the popular hatred of the Church, not to speak of many others who died from the hardships of their prisons.†

* The names of these 16 Jesuits, with their chief places of abode, are given by Father Morris, S.J., in his *Troubles of our Catholic Forefathers*, 1st series, p. 191.

† After the death of Charles II. there was no more blood shed in

In estimating the heroism of our martyrs during this
long and fiery trial, we must not forget what kind of torments were involved in the death which was constantly
before the eyes of the young missioner from the first hour
of his college life.   He had before him the prospect of
being tortured on the rack, suspended above the ground by
the hands in iron gauntlets, bent double in the 'little ease,'
or thrust into loathsome pits.   He had to expect tortures
of the mind as well as of the body, while his persecutors
ply him with insidious questions to draw from him the
names of friends and benefactors which in charity he was
bound to conceal ; and lastly he had to face a death which
was no less than a disgusting and obscene butchery, and of
which the hanging upon the gallows was the least part
either of its shame or of its pain.   With few exceptions the
martyrs were sentenced to the penalty of high treason—to
be hanged, drawn, and quartered.   In some cases indeed
the humanity of the sheriff or the sympathies of the specta-
tors were so far exerted on behalf of the sufferer as to per-
mit him to hang till he was dead ; but commonly the hanging was little more than a rude shock.   It was the knife
and not the rope which was the real instrument of execution.   The body was cut down alive from the gallows, and
then submitted to the barbarous and indescribable process
by which it was ripped up, torn to pieces, and literally, bit

England for the sole cause of religion, but the laws of Elizabeth against
the priesthood remained in full force for nearly another century, and
many of the clergy were tried for their lives for saying Mass.   At the
trial of James Webb, June 25, 1768, the Chief Justice, Lord Mansfield,
had to submit to the jury that it was 'high treason for any man who is
proved to be a priest to breathe in this kingdom' (see Barnard's *Life of
Challoner*, Dublin, 1793).   The last priest tried for his life was the
Hon. and Right Rev. James Talbot, brother of the Earl of Shrewsbury,
at the Old Bailey in 1769, acquitted only for want of evidence.

s during thi
t kind of tor
as constantl
the first hou
· prospect o
ie ground b
'little ease,
pect torture
persecuton
)m him the
arity he wa
death which
hery, and o
· least part
eptions the
reason—to
ses indeed
the specta·
r as to per·
the hang·
the knife
of execu-
llows, and
le process
erally, bit

beth against
entury, and
is. At the
Mansfield,
nan who is
rd's *Life of*
fe was the
irewsbury,
:e.

by bit, thrown into the boiling caldron before the still open eyes of the dying martyr. One instance shall be given in the words of a valiant woman who tells what she saw and heard when, on the 19th of August 1642, Mr. Hugh Green suffered at Dorchester, in the fifty-seventh year of his age. 'The unskilful executioner, by trade a barber,' Mrs. Willoughby writes, 'was so long in dismembering him that he came to his perfect senses and sat upright. The people pulled him down by the rope which was about his neck; then did the butcher cut his belly on both sides and turned the flap upon his breast, which the holy man feeling put his left hand upon his bowels, and looking on his bloody hand laid it down by his side, and lifting up his right hand crossed himself, saying three times, "Jesu, Jesu, Jesu, mercy!" the which, though unworthy, I am witness of, for my hand was on his forehead, and many Protestants heard him and took great notice of it; for all the Catholics were pressed away by the unruly multitude except myself, who never left him until his head was severed from his body. Whilst he was thus calling upon Jesus, the butcher did pull a piece of his liver out instead of his heart, and tumbling the entrails out every way to see if his heart was not amongst them; then with his knife he raked in the body of the blessed martyr, who even then called on Jesus; and his forehead sweat, then it was cold, presently again burned; his eyes, nose, and mouth ran with blood and water. His patience was admirable, and when his tongue could no longer pronounce that life-giving name, Jesu, his lips moved and his inward groans gave signs of those lamentable torments which for more than half an hour he suffered. Methought my heart was pulled out to see him in such cruel pains lifting up his eyes to heaven and not yet dead. Then I could no longer hold, but cried, "Out upon them that did so torment him;" upon which a devout gentlewoman, under-

standing he did yet live, went to Cancola, the sheriff, who
was her uncle's steward, and on her knees besought him to
put him out of his pain, who at her request commanded to
cut off his head.   Then with a knife they did cut his throat,
and with a cleaver chopped off his head ; and so this thrice
most blessed martyr died.'*

Yet it was in anticipation of such an end as this that
young Edmund Genings would speak to his companions at
college, not with fear of the combat, but with eager longing
for his crown, saying, 'Vivamus in spe' (Let us live in hope) !
The manner in which our martyrs prepared for and wel-
comed their death is characteristic throughout.   They met
it not only with Christian patience and fortitude, but with
alacrity and joy.   When Sir Thomas More looked out from
his prison-window upon Father Houghton and his brethren
on the way to their execution, he exclaimed to his daughter,
' See, Meg, these blessed fathers be now as cheerfully going
to their death as bridegrooms to their marriage !'   The same
might have been said of all.   Father Campion used to lift
his hat as he passed under Tyburn gallows, partly out of
reverence for the martyrs who had already shed their blood
there, and partly, as he said, because one day he made sure
he would hang there himself.   Father Bullaker, when he
heard his sentence pronounced, could not contain his joy,
but fell on his knees and sang his *Te Deum* in open court.
At the gallows the most timid by nature seemed to gain
strength at the sight before them.   Those who came last
would embrace the dead and mangled corpses of those who
had gone before, or dip their own rope in the pools of blood,

* This is by no means a solitary instance of such prolonged torture.
A very similar case is described in the 'Life and Martyrdom of Mr.
Richard White, schoolmaster,' protomartyr of Wales, in the *Rambler*
of 1860, vol. iii. p. 233 ; and a number of others may be found in
Challoner's *Missionary Priests.*

or kiss the stains of blood on the hangman's hand. To many a prisoner awaiting his hour of execution, as with S. Ignatius of Antioch, there was but one cause of anxiety—lest at any moment he should be robbed of his martyr's crown. Perhaps no better example could be selected of the spirit which in general animated the whole body of martyrs and confessors than that expressed in the farewell letter of John Duckett to Dr. Richard Smith, Bishop of Chalcedon, written from his prison on the night before his martyrdom (Sept. 7, 1644). Its beautiful simplicity and sublime faith need no comment. It shall be given in full, for every word is matter for a meditation :*

'Most reverend Father in God,—I desire you to give me leave to bid you farewell, seeing it is the last opportunity I shall have in this life of presenting my humble duty to your Lordship. My time is spent and eternity approacheth, not of misery but of joy. I fear not death, nor I contemn not life. If life were my lot, I should endure it patiently; but if death, I shall receive it joyfully, for that Christ is my life and death is my gain. Never since my receiving of holy orders did I so much fear death as I did life, and now, when it approacheth, can I faint? O, no! for the nearer it is at hand the more my soul rejoiceth, and will ever till my life be ended in this happy cause; and then most of all, as I will hope in the mercy of Christ Jesus, for whose sake I suffer. Therefore I beg of your Lordship, and also of those two worthy houses [Douay and Rome], of which I am a most unworthy member, to give God thanks for this great benefit which He mercifully bestows on me, a miserable sinner. Let us all, I beseech you, rejoice and exult in this day which our Lord hath made,

* The original letter is preserved in the archives of the Archdiocese of Westminster.

who be for ever praised of all for time and eternity.—Your Lordship's humble and undeserving servant,

'JOHN DUCKETT.'

On the other hand, the part that the laity of England took in this sanguinary conflict for the faith is worthy to be held in everlasting remembrance. It is consoling and edifying to observe how constantly each band of priests brought to the gallows was accompanied by one or more such faithful companions in martyrdom—their converts, or their hosts and protectors; as if to give proof of how close and affectionate was the union between the pastor and his flock. Some few examples may be here picked out from among many, in illustration of the severity with which the laity of both sexes were treated, and of the various causes for which they gave their lives. Mr. Swallowell, a minister of the English Church, was hanged, drawn, and quartered, simply for becoming a Catholic. William Pikes in 1591 was, for the same capital offence, cut down from the gallows alive and pinned to the ground by the halberts of the sheriff's men, while his heart was cut out with the butcher's knife. Mr. Ashton, a gentleman of Lancashire, was executed for daring to procure from Rome a dispensation to marry his second cousin; and Nicholas Horner, a poor tailor, was horribly racked and tortured, and finally hanged, for making a 'jerkin' for a priest. Carter, a printer, and Webley, a dyer, were hanged; the one for printing, and the other for distributing, Catholic books. Mrs. Clithero, a lady in York, was pressed to death for refusing to plead on the charge of having harboured a priest in her house; and Mrs. Line was flogged, tortured, and hanged for assisting another to escape from his prison. The year 1593, remarkable for being the only one during the last twenty-two years of Elizabeth's reign in which no priest was put to a violent

death, supplies us with a notable instance of the dangers to which a simple layman, zealous for his faith, might at any time be exposed. Four Catholic gentlemen were imprisoned for recusancy in York gaol. A Protestant minister, who happened to be confined in the same prison for some misdemeanour, persuaded them to give him instruction in the truths of the Catholic faith, and afterwards betrayed them for attempting his conversion. For this offence they were brought to trial, condemned, and executed. Two ladies, Mrs. Anne Tesse and Mrs. Bridget Maskew, were at the same time sentenced to be burnt; and though they were afterwards reprieved, they remained ten years in prison.

Meanwhile the Catholics throughout Europe were admiring and envying this renewal in England of the glories of the first age of the Church. Princes and Bishops delighted to show honour to the English student or exile who passed by their way, as martyrs in desire if not in deed. S. Charles Borromeo seemed to bear a particular affection for our suffering countrymen. S. Philip Neri used to embrace the young priests who went from the Roman College to get the old man's blessing before embarking on their perilous journey; and his well-known greeting to them, 'Salvete flores martyrum!' has ever gratefully been remembered by us, and made the name of the Saint specially dear to all English Catholics. The relics of those who shed their blood were eagerly sought for and treasured as relics of saints. Their pictures adorned the walls of churches, and their lives were written for the edification of the faithful. Catholic literature was full of their praises. The great commentator on Holy Scripture, Cornelius à Lapide, when he comes to speak of the Apostle's words in Heb. x. 34, finds the most obvious illustration of this text in the incidents of the Elizabethan persecution then raging, and makes honourable mention of such men as Francis Tregian or of Philip

Howard Earl of Arundel, 'whose deeds have equalled, if not surpassed, in heroism those of the primitive heroes of the Church.' Cardinal Baronius, in like manner, in his revision of the *Roman Martyrology*, cannot touch on S. Thomas of Canterbury without reference to 'the glory of our own age, which has had the happiness of witnessing so many Thomases crowned,' as he dares to say, ' even with a more ample martyrdom.'

These are the men whom God's Providence has raised up amongst us for our example and our delight. They belong to us, and appeal to us, as no others can. Their blood has hallowed the soil on which we stand. Their precious relics are still in abundance preserved in our colleges and convents, and have by constant miracles borne witness to the efficacy of their prayers. One thing alone is wanting to complete their glory and our consolation—that they should be raised upon the altars of the universal Church by a solemn decree of the Sovereign Pontiff. As far back as 1643 Pope Urban VIII. issued a commission to inquire into the cause and manner of their deaths. The seizure of the papers, the execution of Father Bell, O.S.F., one of the persons thus nominated, and the many difficulties of the times, put a stop to further progress in the matter. Two years ago, the Cardinal Archbishop of Westminster, under happier auspices, thought the fitting moment had arrived for once more bringing forward their cause. The ordinary process instituted by his Eminence was completed in due form at the London Oratory, and the acts forwarded to Rome in the summer of 1874, the Rev. F. Morris, S.J., acting as promoter. May we not pray that it may be reserved for our Holy Father, to whom England owes so much, to confer yet one more blessing on our country by the solemn beatification of these our martyrs?

e equalled, i
ive heroes of
ier, in his re-
n S. Thomas
of our own
ng so many
with a more

e has raised
light. They
can. Their
and. Their
in our col-
racles borne
iing alone is
lation—that
ersal Church
As far back
i to inquire
e seizure of
, one of the
ilties of the
itter. Two
ister, under
arrived for
ie ordinary
ted in due
rwarded to
[orris, S.J.,
it may be
d owes so
country by

The total number of martyrs, whose anniversaries are set
iwn in the following Calendar, is 342, of whom 82 suffered
ider Henry VIII., and the remaining 260 in the reigns of
lizabeth and her successors. To these have been added
ie names of about fifty confessors, who during the latter
:riod terminated their lives in prison under the sentence
death, or who died from the effects of cruel usage and in
e odour of sanctity. This list is small indeed in compari-
n with the vast number of such holy confessors, whose
imes are written in heaven, but may never be known on
.rth. Among the few, however, of whom any record now
rtunately exists, those only have been named in the
ilendar who have found a place in Bishop Challoner's
'emoirs of Missionary Priests; and in nearly all cases, both
martyrs and confessors (after the accession of Elizabeth),
iere any difference existed among authorities as to either
mes or dates, those preferred by the Bishop have been
re adopted, as most trustworthy in themselves and
fficient for the purpose of the Calendar.* The cata-
jue of martyrs during the reign of Henry VIII. is some-
iat smaller than that of other hitherto published lists,
t it has been strictly confined to those in whose case
:re is indisputable evidence that they suffered for religion
ly.

At the end of the year the names of some martyrs and
nfessors have been recorded, whose anniversaries could
t be more exactly determined. There has also been
pended a table of the relative numbers of martyrs from

* On the authority of Canon Estcourt and Father Morris (*Troubles*,
series, p. 235), William Way (*alias* Flower) has been distinguished
im William Wigges (*alias* Way), who is omitted by Bishop Challoner;
io on the authority of Mr. Simpson (*Rambler*, 1858, vol. x. p. 327),
ilisbury, and not Chard, is assigned as the place of martyrdom of Mr.
ambley.

the secular clergy, the religious orders, and laity, a list
places where the martyrdoms of the Elizabethan and s
sequent period took place, and a general index of all :
names occurring in the Calendar.

CALENDAR OF MARTYRS.

January.

JAN.		YEAR.
7	EDWARD WATERSON, Secular Priest, hanged at Newcastle-on-Tyne, under Elizabeth . .	1593
11	WILLIAM CARTER, Printer, hanged at Tyburn, under Elizabeth	1584
17	PLACIDUS ADELHAM (or ADLAND), Benedictine, died (under reprieve) in prison, in London . .	1689
21	EDWARD STRANSHAM, Secular Priest, hanged at Tyburn, under Elizabeth	1586
"	NICHOLAS WOODFEN (*alias* WHEELER), Secular Priest, hanged at Tyburn, under Elizabeth .	1586
"	THOMAS REYNOLDS (*alias* GREEN), Secular Priest, hanged at Tyburn, under Charles I. . .	1642
"	BARTHOLOMEW ROE, Benedictine, hanged at Tyburn, under Charles I.	1642
22	WILLIAM PATENSON, Secular Priest, hanged at Tyburn, under Elizabeth	1592
24	WILLIAM IRELAND, Jesuit, hanged at Tyburn, under Charles II.	1679
"	JOHN GROVE, Layman, hanged at Tyburn, under Charles II.	1679
30	RICHARD BRADLEY, Jesuit, died in Manchester gaol before his trial	1646

c

February.

1	HENRY MORSE, Jesuit, hanged at Tyburn during the Civil War	1645
3	JOHN NELSON, Secular Priest, hanged at Tyburn, under Elizabeth	1578
4	JOHN SPEED, Layman, hanged at Durham, under Elizabeth	1594
7	THOMAS SHERWOOD, Layman, hanged at Tyburn, under Elizabeth	1578
11	FRANCIS LEVISON, Franciscan, died in gaol after fourteen months' imprisonment at Worcester .	1680
12	GEORGE HAYDOCK, Secular Priest, hanged at Tyburn, under Elizabeth	1584
,,	JAMES FENN, Secular Priest, hanged at Tyburn, under Elizabeth	1584
,,	THOMAS HEMERFORD, Secular Priest, hanged at Tyburn, under Elizabeth . . .	1584
,,	JOHN NUTTER, Secular Priest, hanged at Tyburn, under Elizabeth	1584
,,	JOHN MUNDEN, Secular Priest, hanged at Tyburn, under Elizabeth	1584
17	WILLIAM RICHARDSON (*alias* ANDERSON), Secular Priest, hanged at Tyburn, under Elizabeth .	1603
18	JOHN PIBUSH, Secular Priest, hanged at St. Thomas's Waterings, under Elizabeth	1601
,,	WILLIAM HARRINGTON, Secular Priest, hanged at Tyburn, under Elizabeth	1594
20	THOMAS PORMORT, Secular Priest, hanged at St. Paul's Churchyard, under Elizabeth . .	1592
21	ROBERT SOUTHWELL, Jesuit, hanged at Tyburn, under Elizabeth	1595
,,	LAWRENCE HILL, Layman, hanged at Tyburn, under Charles II.	1679

P.S.

)urn during
. 16?
at Tyburn,
. . 15?
ham, under
. . 15?
at Tyburn,
. 15?
gaol after
Vorcester . 16?
l at Tyburn,
. . 15?
at Tyburn,
. . 15?
hanged at
. . 15?
it Tyburn,
. . 16
t Tyburn,
. 15?
), Secular
abeth . 16?
Thomas's
. . 16?
anged at
. . 15?
d at St.
. . 15?
Tyburn,
. . 15?
n, under
. . 16?

FEB.		YEAR.
21	ROBERT GREEN, Layman, hanged at Tyburn, under Charles II.	1679
26	ROBERT DRURY, Secular Priest, hanged at Tyburn, under Elizabeth	1601
27	MARK BARKWORTH (*alias* LAMBERT), Benedictine, hanged at Tyburn, under Elizabeth . .	1601
,,	ROGER FILCOCK, Jesuit, hanged at Tyburn, under Elizabeth	1601
,,	ANNE LINE, Gentlewoman, hanged at Tyburn, under Elizabeth	1601
	Some time in February, FRANCIS NEVILL, Jesuit, thrown down-stairs and killed on his apprehension	1679

March.

MAR.		
4	CHRISTOPHER BAYLES, Secular Priest, hanged in Fleet Street, under Elizabeth . . .	1591
,,	NICHOLAS HORNER, Layman, hanged in Smithfield, under Elizabeth	1591
,,	ALEXANDER BLAKE, Layman, hanged in Gray's Inn Lane, under Elizabeth	1591
7	JOHN LARKE, Rector of Chelsea, hanged at Tyburn, under Henry VIII.	1544
,,	JOHN IRELAND, Secular Priest, hanged at Tyburn, under Henry VIII.	1544
,,	GERMAIN GARDINER, Gentleman, hanged at Tyburn, under Henry VIII.	1544
,,	WILLIAM ATKINS, Jesuit, died in prison, under sentence of death, at Stafford . . .	1681

MAR.		YEAR.
11	THOMAS ATKINSON, Secular Priest, hanged at York, under James I.	1616
,,	RICHARD LACY, Jesuit, died in prison in London .	1681
12	PETER WILFORD (Fr. BONIFACE), Benedictine, died in Newgate prison	1646
15	WILLIAM HART, Secular Priest, hanged at York, under Elizabeth	1583
16	JOHN AMIAS, Secular Priest, hanged at York, under Elizabeth	1589
,,	ROBERT DALBY, Secular Priest, hanged at York, under Elizabeth	1589
18	JOHN THULIS, Secular Priest, hanged at Lancaster, under James I.	1616
,,	ROGER WRENNO, Layman, hanged at Lancaster, under James I.	1616
19	THOMAS ASHBEY, Layman, hanged at Tyburn, under Henry VIII.	1544
21	THOMAS PILCHARD, Secular Priest, hanged at Dorchester, under Elizabeth	1587
,,	MATTHEW FLATHERS, Secular Priest, hanged at York, under James I.	1608
22	JAMES HARRISON, Secular Priest, hanged at York, under Elizabeth	1602
,,	ANTHONY BATTIE (or BATES), Layman, hanged at York, under Elizabeth	1602
23	EDMUND SYKES, Secular Priest, hanged at York, under Elizabeth	1587 or 8
25	JAMES BIRD, Gentleman, hanged at Winchester, under Elizabeth	1593
,,	MARGARET CLITHERO, Gentlewoman, pressed to death at York, under Elizabeth . . .	1586
28	CHRISTOPHER WHARTON, Secular Priest, hanged at York, under Elizabeth	1600

Some time during Lent in 1595, JAMES ATKINSON, Layman, killed under torture.

Also, some time in March, THURSTAN HUNT and ROBERT MIDDLETON, Secular Priests, hanged at Lancaster 1601

April.

1 JOHN BRITTON, Gentleman, hanged at York, under Elizabeth 1598

2 JOHN PAINE, Secular Priest, hanged at Chelmsford, under Elizabeth 1582

7 ALEXANDER RAWLINS, Secular Priest, hanged at York, under Elizabeth 1595

,, HENRY WALPOLE, Jesuit, hanged at York, under Elizabeth 1595

,, EDWARD OLDCORNE, Jesuit, hanged at Worcester, under James I. 1606

,, RALPH ASHLEY, Jesuit Lay Brother, hanged at Worcester, under James I. 1606

10 WILLIAM PETERSON, Secular Priest, hanged at Calais, under Henry VIII. 1540

,, WILLIAM RICHARDSON, Secular Priest, hanged at Calais, under Henry VIII. 1540

11 GEORGE GERVAISE, Benedictine, hanged at Tyburn, under James I. 1608

13 JOHN LOCKWOOD (*alias* LASSELS), Secular Priest, hanged at York, under Charles I. . . . 1642

,, EDMUND CATHERICK, Secular Priest, hanged at York, under Charles I. 1642

17 HENRY HEATH, Franciscan, hanged at Tyburn during the Civil War 1643

19 JAMES DUCKETT, Bookseller, hanged at Tyburn, under Elizabeth 1602

APR.		YEAR
20	JAMES BELL, Secular Priest, hanged at Lancaster, under Elizabeth	1584
,,	JOHN FINCH, Layman, hanged at Lancaster, under Elizabeth	1584
,,	RICHARD SERGEANT (*alias* LONG), Secular Priest, hanged at Tyburn, under Elizabeth . .	1586
,,	WILLIAM THOMSON (*alias* BLACKBURN), Secular Priest, hanged at Tyburn, under Elizabeth .	1586
,,	ANTONY PAGE, Secular Priest, hanged at York, under Elizabeth	1593
,,	THOMAS TICHBURN, Secular Priest, hanged at Tyburn, under Elizabeth	1602
,,	ROBERT WATKINSON, Secular Priest, hanged at Tyburn, under Elizabeth	1602
,,	FRANCIS PAGE, Jesuit, hanged at Tyburn, under Elizabeth	1602
25	ROBERT ANDERTON, Secular Priest, hanged in the Isle of Wight, under Elizabeth . . .	1586
,,	WILLIAM MARSDEN, Secular Priest, hanged in the Isle of Wight, under Elizabeth . . .	1586
26	EDWARD MORGAN (*alias* SINGLETON), Secular Priest, hanged at Tyburn, under Charles I. . .	1642
30	MILES GERARD, Secular Priest, hanged at Rochester, under Elizabeth	1590
,,	FRANCIS DICONSON, Secular Priest, hanged at Rochester, under Elizabeth . . .	1590
,,	WILLIAM SOUTHERNE, Secular Priest, hanged at Newcastle-under-Lyne, under James I. . .	1618
	JOHN HAMBLEY, Secular Priest, hanged at Salisbury about Easter, under Elizabeth . .	1587
	Also Mr. WILKS (*alias* TOMSON), a Secular Priest, died in York Castle under sentence of death, shortly after the execution of Mr. Lockwood and Mr. Catherick	1642

ged at Lancaster,
  . . . 1:
Lancaster, under
  . . . 1:
1, Secular Priest,
ibeth . . 1:
KBURN), Secular
er Elizabeth . 15:
d at York, under
  . . . 15
anged at Tyburn,
  . . . 16:
est, hanged al
  . . . 16:
Tyburn, under
  . . . 16:
hanged in the
  . . . 15
hanged in the
  . . . 15
, Secular Priest,
s I. . . 16:
zed at Roches-
  . . . 15
st, hanged at
  . . . 15
anged at New-
  . . . 16:
d at Salisbury
  . . . 15:
secular Priest,
nce of death,
Ir. Lockwood
  . . . 16:

𝕸𝖆𝖞.

MAY.		YEAR.
3	HENRY GARNET, Jesuit, hanged in St. Paul's Church-yard, under James I.	1606
„	NICHOLAS OWEN, Jesuit Lay Brother, died of the rack	1606
4	JOHN HOUGHTON, Prior of the London Charter House, hanged at Tyburn, under Henry VIII. . .	1535
„	AUGUSTINE WEBSTER, Prior of the Carthusian House of Visitation, near Eppeworth, hanged at Tyburn, under Henry VIII. . . .	1535
„	ROBERT LAWRENCE, Carthusian, Prior of Beauvale, Nottinghamshire, hanged at Tyburn, under Henry VIII.	1535
„	RICHARD REYNOLDS, Bridgettine Monk of Sion House, hanged at Tyburn, under Henry VIII.	1535
6	ANTONY MIDDLETON, Secular Priest, hanged at Clerkenwell, under Elizabeth . .	1590
„	EDWARD JONES, Secular Priest, hanged in Fleet Street, under Elizabeth . . .	1590
„	Mr. PRICE of Washingley, shot in cold blood at Lin-coln by the Parliamentary soldiers . .	1644
9	THOMAS PICKERING, Benedictine Lay Brother, hanged at Tyburn, under Charles II. . .	1679
11	JOHN ROCHESTER, Carthusian, hanged in chains at York, under Henry VIII. . . .	1537
„	JAMES WANNERT (or WALWORTH), Carthusian, hanged in chains at York, under Henry VIII.	1537
19	PETER WRIGHT, Jesuit, hanged at Tyburn during the Rebellion	1651
22	JOHN FOREST, Franciscan, burnt at Smithfield, under Henry VIII.	1538
23	BENEDICT (or ROBERT) COX, Benedictine, died under sentence of death in the Clink . .	1650

MAY.		·YEAR.
27	EDMUND DUKE, Secular Priest, hanged at Durham, under Elizabeth	1590
,,	RICHARD HILL, Secular Priest, hanged at Durham, under Elizabeth	1590
,,	JOHN HOG, Secular Priest, hanged at Durham, under Elizabeth	1590
,,	RICHARD HOLIDAY, Secular Priest, hanged at Durham, under Elizabeth	1590
28	THOMAS FORDE, Secular Priest, hanged at Tyburn, under Elizabeth	1582
,,	JOHN SHERT, Secular Priest, hanged at Tyburn, under Elizabeth	1582
,,	ROBERT JOHNSON, Secular Priest, hanged at Tyburn, under Elizabeth	1582
29	RICHARD THIRKHILL (or THIRKELD), Secular Priest, hanged at York, under Elizabeth . . .	1583
30	WILLIAM FILBIE, Secular Priest, hanged at Tyburn, under Elizabeth	1582
,,	LUKE KIRBY, Secular Priest, hanged at Tyburn, under Elizabeth	1582
,,	LAURENCE RICHARDSON (*alias* JOHNSON), Secular Priest, hanged at Tyburn, under Elizabeth .	1582
,,	THOMAS COTTAM, Secular Priest, hanged at Tyburn, under Elizabeth	1582
,,	WILLIAM (or MAURUS) SCOT, Benedictine, hanged at Tyburn, under James I.	1612
,,	RICHARD NEWPORT (*alias* SMITH), Secular Priest, hanged at Tyburn, under James I. . .	1612
31	ROBERT THORPE, Secular Priest, hanged at York, under Elizabeth	1591
,,	THOMAS WATKINSON, Yeoman, hanged (but not quartered) at York, under Elizabeth . .	1591

June.

JUNE.		YEAR.
3	FRANCIS INGOLBY, Secular Priest, hanged at York, under Elizabeth	1586
15	PETER SNOW, Secular Priest, hanged at York, under Elizabeth	1598
"	RALPH GRIMSTON, Gentleman, hanged at York, under Elizabeth	1598
19	WILLIAM EXMEW, Carthusian Monk, hanged at Tyburn, under Henry VIII.	1535
"	HUMPHREY MIDDLEMORE, Carthusian Monk, hanged at Tyburn, under Henry VIII.	1535
"	SEBASTIAN NEWDIGATE, Carthusian Monk, hanged at Tyburn, under Henry VIII.	1535
20	THOMAS WHITEBREAD (*alias* HARCOT), Jesuit, hanged at Tyburn, under Charles II.	1679
"	WILLIAM HARCOURT (*alias* WARING), Jesuit, hanged at Tyburn, under Charles II.	1679
"	JOHN FENWICK, Jesuit, hanged at Tyburn, under Charles II.	1679
"	JOHN GAVAN, Jesuit, hanged at Tyburn, under Charles II.	1679
"	ANTHONY TURNER, Jesuit, hanged at Tyburn, under Charles II.	1679
21	JOHN RIGBY, Layman, hanged at St. Thomas's Waterings, under Elizabeth	1600
22	JOHN FISHER, Bishop of Rochester and Cardinal, beheaded on Tower Hill, under Henry VIII.	1535
23	ROBERT ASHTON, Gentleman, hanged at Tyburn, under Elizabeth	1592
"	THOMAS GARNET, Jesuit, hanged at Tyburn, under James I.	1608
28	JOHN SOUTHWORTH, Secular Priest, hanged at Tyburn during the Commonwealth	1654

JUNE.		YEAR.
30	PHILIP POWEL (*alias* MORGAN), Benedictine, hanged at Tyburn during the Civil Wars . . .	1646

Some time in the latter part of June, under Henry VIII., in 1537, nine Carthusians, viz.
THOMAS JOHNSON, Priest,
RICHARD BERE, Priest,
THOMAS GREENE, Priest,
JOHN DAVY, Professed Monk,
ROBERT SALT, Lay Brother,
WILLIAM GRENEWODE, Lay Brother,
THOMAS REDYNG, Lay Brother,
THOMAS SCRYVEN, Lay Brother,
WALTER PIERSON, Lay Brother,
were killed by slow starvation in Newgate.

Some time in June 1592, THOMAS METHAM, Jesuit, died in Wisbeach Castle, a prisoner for the Faith.

July.

JULY.		
I	Sir DAVID GUNSTON (or GENSON), Knight of St. John, beheaded at St. Thomas's Waterings, under Henry VIII.	1541
,,	THOMAS MAXFIELD, Secular Priest, hanged at Tyburn, under James I.	1616
,,	OLIVER PLUNKET, Archbishop of Armagh, hanged at Tyburn, under Charles II. . . .	1681
2	MONFORD SCOT, Secular Priest, hanged in Fleet Street, under Elizabeth	1591
,,	GEORGE BEESLEY, Secular Priest, hanged in Fleet Street, under Elizabeth	1591
4	JOHN CORNELIUS (*alias* MOHUN), Jesuit, hanged at Dorchester, under Elizabeth	1594
,,	THOMAS BOSGRAVE, Gentleman, hanged at Dorchester, under Elizabeth	1594

CALE

JOHN CAREY, La
Elizabeth

PATRICK SALMO
under Eliza

WILLIAM ANDLI
under Eliza

THOMAS WARC(
Elizabeth

EDWARD FULT
Elizabeth

GEORGE NICOL
under Eli

RICHARD YAXI
under Eli

THOMAS BELS
Elizabeth

HUMPHREY P
under El

Sir THOMAS
Hill, un

THOMAS ALF
under E

THOMAS WEI
Elizabet

ROGER DIC
chester,

RALPH MIL
under

Sir ADRIAN
rusalen
VIII.

Sir THOMAS
lem, t
VIII.

IRTYRS.

enedictine, hanged
Vars . . . *16*

une, under Henry
ians, viz.

onk,
er,
ty Brother,
other,
rother,
other,
in Newgate.
METHAM, Jesuit,
oner for the Faith.

ight of St. John,
aterings, under
. . . *1511*

nged at Tyburn,
. . . *1616*

rmagh, hanged
. . . *1681*

nged in Fleet
. . . *1591*

anged in Fleet
. . . *1591*

uit, hanged at
. . . *1594*

ged at Dor-
. . . *1594*

t.		YEAR.
	JOHN CAREY, Layman, hanged at Dorchester, under Elizabeth	1594
	PATRICK SALMON, Layman, hanged at Dorchester, under Elizabeth	1594
	WILLIAM ANDLEBY, Secular Priest, hanged at York, under Elizabeth	1597
	THOMAS WARCOP, Layman, hanged at York, under Elizabeth	1597
	EDWARD FULTHORP, Layman, hanged at York, under Elizabeth	1597
	GEORGE NICOLS, Secular Priest, hanged at Oxford, under Elizabeth	1589
	RICHARD YAXLEY, Secular Priest, hanged at Oxford, under Elizabeth	1589
	THOMAS BELSON, Layman, hanged at Oxford, under Elizabeth	1589
	HUMPHREY PRICHARD, Layman, hanged at Oxford, under Elizabeth	1589
	Sir THOMAS MORE, Chancellor, beheaded on Tower Hill, under Henry VIII. . . .	1535
	THOMAS ALFIELD, Secular Priest, hanged at Tyburn, under Elizabeth	1585
	THOMAS WEBLEY, Layman, hanged at Tyburn, under Elizabeth	1585
	ROGER DICONSON, Secular Priest, hanged at Winchester, under Elizabeth	1591
	RALPH MILNER, Layman, hanged at Winchester, under Elizabeth	1591
	Sir ADRIAN FORTESCUE, Knight of St. John of Jerusalem, beheaded on Tower Hill, under Henry VIII.	1539
	Sir THOMAS DINGLEY, Prior of St. John of Jerusalem, beheaded on Tower Hill, under Henry VIII.	1539

JULY.		YEAR.
8	JOHN GRIFFITH, Vicar of Wandsworth, hanged at St. Thomas's Waterings, under Henry VIII. .	1539
,,	N. WAIRE, Franciscan, hanged at St. Thomas's Waterings, under Henry VIII. . . .	1539
12	JOHN JONES (alias BUCKLEY), Franciscan, hanged at St. Thomas's Waterings, under Elizabeth .	1598
13	THOMAS TUNSTAL (alias HELMES), Secular Priest, hanged at Norwich, under James I. . .	1616
14	RICHARD LANGHORNE, Barrister, hanged at Tyburn, under Charles II.	1679
16	JOHN LION, Yeoman, hanged at Oakham in Rutland, under Elizabeth	1599
,,	JOHN SUGAR, Secular Priest, hanged at Warwick, under James I.	1604
,,	ROBERT GRISSOLD (or GRESWOLD), hanged at Warwick, under James I.	1604
19	ANTONY BROOKBY, Franciscan, strangled with his own girdle in prison, under Henry VIII. .	1537
,,	WILLIAM PLESSINGTON, Secular Priest, hanged at Chester, under Charles II.	1679
22	PHILIP EVANS, Jesuit, hanged at Cardiff, under Charles II.	1679
,,	JOHN LLOYD, Secular Priest, hanged at Cardiff, under Charles II.	1679
24	NICHOLAS GARLICK, Secular Priest, hanged at Derby, under Elizabeth	1588
,,	ROBERT LUDLAM, Secular Priest, hanged at Derby, under Elizabeth	1588
,,	RICHARD SYMPSON, Secular Priest, hanged at Derby, under Elizabeth	1588
,,	JOHN BOST, Secular Priest, hanged at Durham, under Elizabeth	1594
25	JOHN INGRAM, Secular Priest, hanged at Newcastle, under Elizabeth	1594

JULY.		YEAR.
26	GEORGE SWALLOWELL, converted minister, hanged at Darlington, under Elizabeth . . .	1594
„	ROBERT NUTTER, Secular Priest, hanged at Lancaster, under Elizabeth	1600
„	EDWARD THWING, Secular Priest, hanged at Lancaster, under Elizabeth	1600
„	WILLIAM WARD (*alias* WEBSTER), Secular Priest, hanged at Tyburn, under Charles I. . .	1641
„	BONIFACE KEMPE, Benedictine, died of cruel usage during the Civil Wars	1644
„	ILDEPHONSE HESKETH, Benedictine, died of cruel usage during the Civil Wars . . .	1644
27	THOMAS CORT, Franciscan, starved to death in prison, under Henry VIII.	1538
„	ROBERT SUTTON, Secular Priest, hanged at Stafford, under Elizabeth	1587
„	WILLIAM DAVIES, Secular Priest, hanged at Beaumaris, under Elizabeth	1592
„	JOSEPH LAMPTON, Secular Priest, hanged at Newcastle, under Elizabeth	1593
30	JOHN TRAVERS, D.D., Secular Priest, executed at London, under Henry VIII. . . .	1539
„	THOMAS ABELL, Secular Priest, hanged at Smithfield, under Henry VIII.	1540
„	EDWARD POWELL, Secular Priest, hanged at Smithfield, under Henry VIII.	1540
„	RICHARD FETHERSTONE, Secular Priest, hanged at Smithfield, under Henry VIII. . . .	1540
31	EVERARD HANSE, Secular Priest, hanged at Tyburn, under Elizabeth	1581
	Some time in July, THOMAS SPROTT and THOMAS HUNT, Secular Priests, hanged at Lincoln, under Elizabeth . . ·. . .	1600

𝔄𝔲𝔤𝔲𝔰𝔱.

AUG.		YEAR.
1	THOMAS WELBOURNE, Layman, hanged at York, under James I.	1605
,,	JOHN FULTHERING, Layman, hanged at York, under James I.	1605
3	THOMAS BELCHIAM, Franciscan, starved to death in the Tower, under Henry VIII. . . .	1538
4	EDMUND BRINDHOLME, Secular Priest, hanged at Tyburn, under Henry VIII.	1540
,,	WILLIAM HORNE, Carthusian Lay Brother, hanged at Tyburn, under Henry VIII. . . .	1540
,,	CLEMENT PHILPOT, Gentleman, hanged at Tyburn, under Henry VIII.	1540
,,	GILES HERON, Gentleman, hanged at Tyburn, under Henry VIII.	1540
7	EDWARD BAMBER (or REDING), Secular Priest, hanged at Lancaster during the Civil War	1646
,,	JOHN WOODCOCK (*alias* FARINGDON), Franciscan, hanged at Lancaster during the Civil War	1646
,,	THOMAS WHITAKER, Secular Priest, hanged at Lancaster during the Civil War . . .	1646
,,	NICHOLAS POSTGATE, Secular Priest, hanged at York, under Charles II.	1679
8	JOHN FINGLOW (or FINGLEY), Secular Priest, hanged at York, under Elizabeth . . .	1586 or 7
9	THOMAS PALASOR, Secular Priest, hanged at Durham, under Elizabeth	1600
,,	JOHN NORTON, Gentleman, hanged at Durham, under Elizabeth	1600
,,	JOHN TALBOT, Gentleman, hanged at Durham, under Elizabeth	1600

AUG.		YEAR.
11	JOHN SANDYS, Secular Priest, hanged at Gloucester, under Elizabeth	1586
12	CHARLES MAHONY, Franciscan, hanged at Ruthin, under Charles II.	1679
13	WILLIAM FREEMAN (*alias* MASON), Secular Priest, hanged at Warwick, under Elizabeth . .	1595
,,	JAMES DOUDAL, Irish Merchant, hanged at Exeter, under Elizabeth	1599
19	CHRISTOPHER ROBINSON, Secular Priest, hanged at Carlisle, under Elizabeth	1598
,,	HUGH GREEN (*alias* F. BROOKS), Secular Priest, hanged at Dorchester during the Civil War .	1642
22	WILLIAM LACY, Secular Priest, hanged at York, under Elizabeth	1582
,,	RICHARD KIRKEMAN, Secular Priest, hanged at York, under Elizabeth	1582
,,	JOHN KEMBLE, Secular Priest, hanged at Hereford, under Charles II.	1679
,,	JOHN WALL (*alias* FRANCIS JOHNSON), Franciscan, hanged at Worcester, under Charles II. .	1679
24	NICHOLAS TICHBURN, Gentleman, hanged at Tyburn, under Elizabeth	1601
,,	THOMAS HACKSHOT, Layman, hanged at Tyburn, under Elizabeth	1601
27	ROGER CADWALLADOR, Secular Priest, hanged at Leominster, under James I.	1610
,,	CHARLES BAKER (*alias* DAVID LEWIS), Jesuit, hanged at Usk, under Charles II. . . .	1679
28	WILLIAM DEAN, Secular Priest, hanged at Miles End Green, under Elizabeth . . .	1588
,,	HENRY WEBLEY, Layman, hanged at Miles End Green, under Elizabeth . . .	1588

AUG.		YEAR.
28	WILLIAM GUNTER, Secular Priest, hanged at the Theatre, under Elizabeth . . ,	1588
,,	ROBERT MORTON, Secular Priest, hanged at Lincoln's Inn Fields, under Elizabeth . .	1588
,,	HUGH MOOR, Gentleman, hanged at Lincoln's Inn Fields, under Elizabeth . . .	1588
,,	THOMAS HOLFORD (*alias* ACTON), Secular Priest, hanged at Clerkenwell, under Elizabeth	1588
,,	JAMES CLAXTON (or CLARKSON), Secular Priest, hanged near Hounslow, under Elizabeth	1588
,,	THOMAS FELTON, Gentleman, hanged near Hounslow, under Elizabeth	1588
,,	EDMUND ARROWSMITH, Jesuit, hanged at Lancaster, under Charles I.	1628
29	RICHARD HERST, Layman, hanged at Lancaster, under Charles I.	1628
30	RICHARD LEIGH, Secular Priest, hanged at Tyburn, under Elizabeth	1588
,,	EDWARD SHELLEY, Gentleman, hanged at Tyburn, under Elizabeth	1588
,,	RICHARD MARTIN, Layman, hanged at Tyburn, under Elizabeth	1588
,,	RICHARD FLOWER, Layman, hanged at Tyburn, under Elizabeth	1588
,,	JOHN ROCH, Layman, hanged at Tyburn, under Elizabeth	1588
,,	Mrs. MARGARET WARD, hanged at Tyburn, under Elizabeth	1588

Some time in August 1583, thirty-two Franciscans dispersed through the country in various prisons, and there starved to death.

RTYRS.

t, hanged at the
. , . 15ᵗ

hanged at Lin-
beth . . . 15ᵗ

at Lincoln's Inn
. . 15ᵗ

, Secular Priest,
Elizabeth . 15ᵗ

, Secular Priest,
r Elizabeth . 15ᵗ

ged near Houns-
. . 15ᵗ

ged at Lancaster,
. . . 16ᵗ

d at Lancaster,
. . . 16ᵗ

nged at Tyburn,
. . . 15ᵗ

nged at Tyburn,
. . . 15ᵗ

ged at Tyburn,
. . . 15ᵗ

ged at Tyburn,
. . . 15ᵗ

Tyburn, under
. . . 15ᵗ

Tyburn, under
. . 15ᵗ

wo Franciscans
in various pri-

.

September.

SEPT.		YEAR.
4	RICHARD HORNER, Secular Priest, hanged at York, under Elizabeth	1598
5	WILLIAM BROWN, Layman, hanged at Ripon, under James I.	1605
7	JOHN DUCKETT, Secular Priest, hanged at Tyburn during the Civil War	1644
„	RALPH CORBY, Jesuit, hanged at Tyburn during the Civil War	1644
9	GEORGE DOUGLAS, Secular Priest of Scotland, hanged at York, under Elizabeth . . .	1587
10	EDWARD BARLOW, Benedictine, hanged at Lancaster, under Charles I.	1641
16	LAURENCE BAILY, Layman, hanged at Lancaster, under James I.	1604
23	WILLIAM WAY (*alias* FLOWER), Secular Priest, hanged at Kingston-on-Thames, under Elizabeth .	1588
24	WILLIAM SPENSER, Secular Priest, hanged at York, under Elizabeth	1589
„	ROBERT HARDESTY, Layman, hanged at York, under Elizabeth	1589
25	FRANCIS TREGIAN, after release from twenty-five years' imprisonment, died at Lisbon . .	1608
27	THOMAS JENISON, Jesuit, died in gaol after a year's imprisonment	1679

D

⦿ctober.

OCT.		YEAR.
I	ROBERT WILCOX, Secular Priest, hanged at Canterbury, under Elizabeth	1588
,,	EDWARD CAMPIAN, Secular Priest, hanged at Canterbury, under Elizabeth	1588
,,	CHRISTOPHER BUXTON, Secular Priest, hanged at Canterbury, under Elizabeth . . .	1588
,,	ROBERT WIDMERPOOL, Gentleman, hanged at Canterbury, under Elizabeth	1588
,,	RALPH CROKETT, Secular Priest, hanged at Chichester, under Elizabeth	1588
,,	EDWARD JAMES, Secular Priest, hanged at Chichester, under Elizabeth	1588
,,	JOHN ROBINSON, Secular Priest, hanged at Ipswich, under Elizabeth	1588
,,	WILLIAM WIGGES, Secular Priest, hanged at Kingston-on-Thames, under Elizabeth . .	1588
5	WILLIAM HARTLEY, Secular Priest, hanged near the Theatre, London, under Elizabeth . .	1588
,,	JOHN WELDON, Secular Priest, hanged at Miles End Green, under Elizabeth . . .	1588
,,	RICHARD WILLIAMS, Secular Priest, hanged at Holloway, under Elizabeth . . .	1588
,,	ROBERT SUTTON, Schoolmaster, hanged at Clerkenwell, under Elizabeth	1588
,,	JOHN HEWETT, Secular Priest, hanged at York, under Elizabeth	1588
8	JOHN LOWE, Secular Priest, hanged at Tyburn, under Elizabeth	1586
,,	JOHN ADAMS, Secular Priest, hanged at Tyburn, under Elizabeth	1586

RICHARD (or I
hanged at

ROBERT BICKE
under Eliz

THOMAS BULL
during the

MATTHEW AT
Castle, af

RICHARD WH
ham, und

PHILIP HOWA
after ele
beth .

THOMAS TH
under C

JOHN SLADE,
under E

JOHN BODY
Elizab

GEORGE N
under

ROBERT W
hange

JOHN THC
tonbu

ROGER JA
tonbu

HUGH F
Read

OCT.   YEAR.

8   RICHARD (or ROBERT) DIBDALE, Secular Priest, hanged at Tyburn, under Elizabeth . . 1586

„   ROBERT BICKERDIKE, Gentleman, hanged at York, under Elizabeth . . . . . 1585 or 6

12   THOMAS BULLAKER, Franciscan, hanged at Tyburn during the Civil War 1642

15   MATTHEW ATKINSON, Franciscan, died in Hurst Castle, after thirty years' imprisonment . . 1729

17   RICHARD WHITE, Schoolmaster, hanged at Wrexham, under Elizabeth 1584

19   PHILIP HOWARD, Earl of Arundel, died in the Tower, after eleven years' imprisonment, under Elizabeth 1595

23   THOMAS THWING, Secular Priest, hanged at York, under Charles II. 1680

30   JOHN SLADE, Schoolmaster, hanged at Winchester, under Elizabeth 1583

November.

NOV.

2   JOHN BODY, Gentleman, hanged at Andover, under Elizabeth 1583

9   GEORGE NAPPIER, Secular Priest, hanged at Oxford, under James I. 1610

15   ROBERT WHITING, Abbot of Glastonbury, O.S.B., hanged at Glastonbury, under Henry VIII. . 1539

„   JOHN THORNE, Benedictine Monk, hanged at Glastonbury, under Henry VIII. 1539

„   ROGER JAMES, Benedictine Monk, hanged at Glastonbury, under Henry VIII. . . . 1539

„   HUGH FARINGDON, Abbot of Reading, hanged at Reading, under Henry VIII. . . . 1539

NOV.		YEAR.
15	JOHN RUGGE, Secular Priest, hanged at Reading, under Henry VIII.	1539
,,	WILLIAM ONION, Secular Priest, hanged at Reading, under Henry VIII.	1539
16	EDWARD OSBALDESTON, Secular Priest, hanged at York, under Elizabeth	1594
26	HUGH TAYLOR, Secular Priest, hanged at York, under Elizabeth	1585
,,	MARMADUKE BOWES, Gentleman, hanged at York, under Elizabeth	1585
28	JAMES THOMPSON, Secular Priest, hanged at York, under Elizabeth	1582
29	CUTHBERT MAINE, Secular Priest, hanged at Launceston, under Elizabeth . . .	1577
,,	EDWARD BURDEN, Secular Priest, hanged at York, under Elizabeth	1588
,,	GEORGE ERRINGTON, Gentleman, hanged at York, under Elizabeth	1596
,,	WILLIAM KNIGHT, Yeoman, hanged at York, under Elizabeth	1596
,,	WILLIAM GIBSON, Yeoman, hanged at York, under Elizabeth	1596
,,	HENRY ABBOT, Yeoman, hanged at York, under Elizabeth	1596
30	ALEXANDER CROW, Secular Priest, hanged at York, under Elizabeth	1586 or 7

In November 1584, ROGER WAKEMAN, Secular Priest, died from the filth of his prison, after two years in Newgate.

JOHN BECH
under

EDMUND C
Elizal

RALPH SHI
under

ALEXANDE
undei

RICHARD
unde:

EDWARD
unde

EDWARD
gate

JOHN A
han

EDMUND
lnn

SWITHIN
Fie

POLYDO
bu

EUSTAC
bu

BRYAN
El

JOHN
E:

December.

DEC.		YEAR.
1	JOHN BECHE, Abbot of Colchester, O.S.B., executed, under Henry VIII.	1539
"	EDMUND CAMPION, Jesuit, hanged at Tyburn, under Elizabeth	1581
"	RALPH SHERWINE, Secular Priest, hanged at Tyburn, under Elizabeth	1581
"	ALEXANDER BRIANT, Jesuit, hanged at Tyburn, under Elizabeth	1581
"	RICHARD LANGLEY, Gentleman, hanged at York, under Elizabeth	1586
3	EDWARD COLEMAN, Gentleman, hanged at Tyburn, under Charles II.	1678
"	EDWARD MICO, Jesuit, died from ill-usage in Newgate	1678
5	JOHN ALMOND (*alias* LATHOM), Secular Priest, hanged at Tyburn, under James I.	1612
10	EDMUND GENINGS, Secular Priest, hanged at Gray's Inn Fields, under Elizabeth	1591
"	SWITHIN WELLS, Gentleman, hanged at Gray's Inn Fields, under Elizabeth	1591
"	POLYDORE PLASDEN, Secular Priest, hanged at Tyburn, under Elizabeth	1591
"	EUSTACHIUS WHITE, Secular Priest, hanged at Tyburn, under Elizabeth	1591
"	BRYAN LACY, Gentleman, hanged at Tyburn, under Elizabeth	1591
"	JOHN MASON, Layman, hanged at Tyburn, under Elizabeth	1591

DEC.		YEAR.
10	SYDNEY HODGSON, Layman, hanged at Tyburn, under Elizabeth	1591
,,	JOHN ROBERTS, Benedictine, hanged at Tyburn, under James I.	1610
,,	THOMAS SOMERS (*alias* WILSON), Secular Priest, hanged at Tyburn, under James I. . .	1610
11	ARTHUR BELL, Franciscan, hanged at Tyburn during the Civil War	1643
,,	BENNET CONSTABLE, Benedictine, died in Durham gaol	1683
12	THOMAS HOLLAND, Jesuit, hanged at Tyburn during the Civil War	1642
21	THOMAS MOMFORD (*alias* BEDINGFIELD), died at the Gatehouse	1678
24	GEORGE MUSCOT, Secular Priest, after twenty years' imprisonment, died at Douay . .	1645
29	WILLIAM HOWARD, Viscount Stafford, beheaded on Tower Hill, under Charles II. . .	1680

MARTY

WHOSE ANNIVER:

HS STONE, Augu
  Henry VIII.,
EPHEN ROUSHA?
  Elizabeth, in
ILLIAM LAMPLE
  Elizabeth, so
ILLIAM PIKES, I
  beth, some ti
ATTHIAS HARR:
  Elizabeth, in
WRENCE HUN
  under Elizal
MES MAWSON,
  in 1612.
HOMAS DYER,
  James I., b
uring the Eli

ILLIAM CHAPI
HOMAS COTES
WARD POLE,
WRENCE VA
  Canon Re

MARTYRS AND CONFESSORS

WHOSE ANNIVERSARIES HAVE NOT BEEN MORE PRECISELY
ASCERTAINED.

———

JOHN STONE, Augustinian Friar, executed at Canterbury, under
Henry VIII., some time in 1538.

STEPHEN ROUSHAM, Secular Priest, hanged at Gloucester, under
Elizabeth, in March or July 1587.

WILLIAM LAMPLEY, Layman, hanged at Gloucester, under
Elizabeth, some time in 1588.

WILLIAM PIKES, Layman, hanged at Dorchester, under Elizabeth, some time in 1591.

MATTHIAS HARRISON, Secular Priest, hanged at York, under
Elizabeth, in 1591.

LAWRENCE HUMPHREYS, Layman, hanged at Winchester,
under Elizabeth, in 1591.

JAMES MAWSON, Layman, hanged at Tyburn, under James I.,
in 1612.

THOMAS DYER, Benedictine, hanged (locality unknown), under
James I., between 1618 and 1624.

During the Elizabethan persecution there perished in prison
as confessors of the faith :

WILLIAM CHAPLAIN, Secular Priest, in 1583.

THOMAS COTESMORE, Secular Priest, in 1584.

EDWARD POLE, Secular Priest, in 1585.

LAWRENCE VAUX, Fellow of Manchester College, afterwards
Canon Regular of St. Augustine, in the Clink.

THOMAS CROWTHER, Secular Priest, in the Marshalsea, in 1585.

JOHN HARRISON, Secular Priest, in 1586.

MARTIN SHERTON, Secular Priest, in 1587.

Mr. GABRIEL THIMELBY, Gentleman, in 1587.

Mrs. WELLS, in Newgate, under sentence of death, after ten
years' imprisonment, in 1602..

Also during the same period :

Mr. ROBERT HOLMES, Secular Priest.

Mr. JOHN JETTER, Secular Priest.

Mr. JAMES LOMAX, Secular Priest.

Mr. AILWORTH, an Irish Gentleman.

Mr. WILLIAM TYRWHIT, Gentleman.

Mr. DYMOCK, Champion of England.

Mr. CHRISTOPHER WATSON, Layman, and twenty other Catholics, in York prison.

Mr. SHELLEY, Gentleman, in the Marshalsea.

Mr. JOHN COOPER, through cruel treatment, in Beauchamp
Tower.

ELEANORE HUNT, who was sentenced to death for harbouring
a priest, and died, under reprieve, in prison.

During the Parliamentary persecution commenced in the
reign of Charles I. :

F. LAWRENCE MABBS, Benedictine, died in Newgate, in 1641.

JOHN TURNER, Secular Priest, condemned December 8, 1641,
died afterwards in Newgate.

HENRY MYNERS, Secular Priest, condemned at the same time,
died, after many years' imprisonment, in Newgate.

WALTER COLEMAN, Franciscan, died in Newgate, in 1645.

JOHN GOODMAN, Secular Priest, died in Newgate, in 1645.

BRIAN CANSFIELD, Jesuit, died in Newgate, in 1645.

JOHN FELTON, Jesuit, within a month after his release from
a cruel imprisonment.

THOMAS VAUGHAN, Secular Priest, died of cruel usage at Cardiff, though not in prison.

THOMAS BLOUNT, Secular Priest, died in Shrewsbury gaol, in 1647.

During the persecution raised by the Oates Plot, in addition to those already enumerated in the Calendar, there perished in prison :

EDWARD TURNER, Jesuit, in London, 1691.

WILLIAM BENNET, Jesuit, at Leicester, in 1691.

RICHARD BIRKET, Secular Priest, under sentence of death, at Lancaster.

WILLIAM LLOYD, Secular Priest, also under sentence of death, six days before the appointed time for his execution, at Brecknock in South Wales.

WILLIAM ALLISON, Secular Priest, in York Castle, at some time during the same period.

ANALYSIS OF THE CATALOGUE OF MARTYRS.

Reign of Henry VIII.		*Reign of Elizabeth, and later.*	
Secular Priests .	. 12	Secular Priests .	. 146
Augustinian . .	. 1	Benedictines .	. 8
Benedictines . .	. 5	Franciscans . .	. 7
Bridgettine . .	. 1	Jesuits . . .	. 23
Carthusians . .	. 12	Laymen (including one	
Franciscans . .	. 37	Benedictine and one	
Laymen (including six		Jesuit Lay Brother) .	73
Carthusian Brothers) .	14	Women . .	. 3
	82		260

PLACES OF EXECUTION,

WITH THE NUMBER OF MARTYRDOMS WHICH TOOK PLACE AT
EACH AFTER THE ACCESSION OF ELIZABETH.

———

Archdiocese of Westminster.

Chelmsford . . .	1
Clerkenwell . . .	3
Fleet Street . . .	4
Gray's Inn Lane . .	3
Holloway . . .	1
Hounslow . . .	2
Lincoln's Inn Fields .	2
Mile's End Green . .	3
St. Paul's Churchyard .	2
Smithfield . . .	1
The Theatre . .	2
Tower Hill . . .	1
Tyburn . . .	90
	115

Diocese of Beverley.

Ripon . . .	1
York . . .	50
	51

Diocese of Birmingham.

Newcastle-under-Lyne .	1
Oxford . . .	5
Stafford . . .	1
Warwick . . .	3
Worcester . . .	3
	13

Diocese of Clifton.

Gloucester . . .	3
Salisbury . . .	1
	4

Diocese of Hexham and Newcastle.

Carlisle . .	1
Darlington . .	1
Durham . .	9
Newcastle-on-Tyne	3
	14

Diocese of
Lancaster .
Diocese of
Men
Cardiff
Hereford
Leominster .
York .

Diocese of .
Ipswich
Norwich

Diocese of
Derby .
Lincoln
Oakham

Dioces.
Dorchester
Exeter
Launceston

XECUTION,

OMS WHICH TOOK PLACE AT
;ION OF ELIZABETH.

—

Diocese of Birmingham.

'ewcastle-under-Lyne . 1
xford . . . ;
:afford . . . 1
'arwick . . . ;
'orcester . . . ;
—
1;

Diocese of Clifton.

oucester . . . ;
lisbury . . . 1

Diocese of Hexham and Newcastle.

rlisle . . . 1
rlington . . .
rham . . . (
wcastle-on-Tyne . ;
—
1.

Diocese of Liverpool.	
Lancaster . . .	15

Diocese of Newport and Menevia.	
Cardiff . . .	2
Hereford . . .	1
Leominster . . .	1
Usk . . .	1
	—
	5

Diocese of Northampton.	
Ipswich . . .	1
Norwich . . .	1
	—
	2

Diocese of Nottingham.	
Derby . . .	3
Lincoln . . .	2
Oakham . . .	1
	—
	6

Diocese of Plymouth.	
Dorchester . . .	7
Exeter . . .	1
Launceston . . .	1
	—
	9

Diocese of Shrewsbury.	
Beaumaris .	1
Chester .	1
Ruthin .	1
Wrexham .	1
	—
	4

Diocese of Southwark.	
Andover . . .	1
Canterbury . . .	4
Chichester . . .	2
Kingston . . .	2
Isle of Wight . . .	2
Rochester . . .	2
St. Thomas's Waterings.	3
Winchester . . .	5
	—
	21

Locality doubtful . . .	1

Total, 260

INDEX OF NAMES.

Thompson, J., Nov. 28.
Thomson, Wm., April 20.
Thorne, J., Nov. 15.
Thorpe, R., May 31.
Thulis, J., March 18.
Thwing, Edw., July 26.
,, Thos., Oct. 28.
Tichburn, Nic., Aug. 24.
,, Thos, April 20.
Tomson, see Wilks.
Travers, J., July 30.
Tregian, T., Sept. 25.
Tunstal, T., July 13.
Turner, Ant., June 20.
,, Edw., p. 41.
,, John, p. 40.
Tyrwhit, W., p. 40.

Vaughan, T., p. 41.
Vaux, L., p. 39.

Waire, N., July 8.
Wakeman, R., p. 36.
Wall, J., Aug. 22.
Walpole, R., April 7.
Wannert or Walworth, J.,
  May 11.
Warcop, T., July 4.
Ward, Mrs., Aug. 30.
,, Wm., July 26.
Waring, see Harcourt.
Waterson, E., Jan. 7.

Watkinson, Rob., April 20.
,, Thos., May 31.
Watson, C., p. 40.
Way, Wm., Sept. 23.
Webley, Hen., Aug. 28.
,, Thos., July 6.
Webster, Aug., May 4.
,, see W. Ward.
Welbourne, T., Aug. 1.
Weldon, J., Oct. 5.
Wells, Mrs., p. 40.
,, S., Dec. 10.
Wharton, C., March 28.
Wheeler, see Woodfen.
Whitaker, T., Aug. 7.
White, Eust., Dec. 10.
,, Rich., Oct. 17.
Whitebread, T., June 20.
Whiting, R., Nov. 15.
Widmerpool, R., Oct. 1.
Wigges, W., Oct. 1.
Wilcox, R., Oct. 1.
Wilford, P., March 12.
Wilks, Mr., p. 22.
Williams, R., Oct. 5.
Wilson, see Somers.
Woodcock, J., Aug. 7.
Woodfen, N., Jan. 21.
Wrenno, R., March 18.
Wright, P., May 19.

Yaxley, R., July 5.

LONDON:
ROBSON AND SONS, PRINTERS, PANCRAS ROAD, N.W.

www.ingramcontent.com/pod-product-compliance
Lightning Source LLC
Chambersburg PA
CBHW022037080426
42733CB00007B/872